CATS

Mystical Guide

First English edition, 2026

First printing

ISBN: 978-0-7387-8425-0

Library of Congress Cataloging-in-Publication Data: Pending
Original Italian Edition:

Publisher
Balthazar Pagani

Graphic design and layout
Bebung

Editing and fact-checking
Fabia Brustia

Contents and research by BesideBooks srl

Translation: Qontent
Editing: Phillip Gaskill

20123 Milan, Italy
www.whitestar.it

Llewellyn Publications

A Division of Llewellyn Worldwide Ltd.
2143 Wooddale Drive
Woodbury, MN 55125-2090
www.llewellyn.com

Printed in China

GPSR Representation

UPI-2M PLUS d.o.o., Meduliceva 20 10000 Zagreb, Croatia

matt.parsons@upi2mbooks.hr

MIX
Paper | Supporting responsible forestry
FSC® C178000
FSC www.fsc.org

CATS
Mystical Guide

Magic, Wisdom, and Powers of Feline Breeds

INTRODUCTIONS BY
Ewa Princi and Federica Vanini

ILLUSTRATIONS BY
Fabiana Belmonte

LLEWELLYN
WOODBURY, MINNESOTA

Table of Contents

Editorial note

This book is born from a profound love for animals, and in particular for cats. Every breed explained here has been carefully researched, designed to offer reliable and accessible information to those who want to know more about these wonderful companions.

Along with the historical, etiological, and behavioral data, you will find a part dedicated to magic: a symbolic and imaginative dimension, made of intuitions, associations, and free interpretations. These similarities do not presume to be absolute truths, but small bridges between worlds.

We have tried to discuss every cat with respect and poetry, in the hope that among these pages you will be able to recognize your feline, discover something more about someone who already accompanies you . . . or let you be inspired to meet the right cat, the one that resembles you or completes you. And if in all this, there were also a little magic, let it be yours!

When the Cat Has Chosen the Human

It all started about 9,000 years ago, when a small wild feline—*Felis silvestris lybica* (African Wildcat)—approached the first agricultural villages of the Middle East, attracted by the rodents in the barns. No one imagined that from that meeting one of the deepest bonds between different species would develop.

Since then, the cat has crossed human history: companion of farmers and queens, today it is part of our daily lives, while preserving an unshakable wild soul.

The cat was never domesticated in the classic sense: it was the one who chose to stay, maintaining its own independent nature intact. This is what makes its presence in our lives special. It does not belong to us, yet it accompanies us. It does not serve us, yet it takes care of us. It does not obey us, but watches us and sometimes teaches us.

Every feline breed tells a unique story, but the differences in temperament we observe between one cat and the other are not by chance: they are rooted in three great forces, profoundly interwoven together.

The first force is selective genetics. The breeds that we know today are the results of selections made by man, often starting from natural populations. Breeding has shaped not only the exterior aspect but also the character. Some breeds have been deliberately directed toward more docile and sociable traits, such as the Ragdoll, the Persian, and the Sacred Cat of Burma; others have kept a more pronounced vivacity, an instinctive curiosity, a greater need for exploration, such as the Bengal, the Abyssinian, the Siamese.

The second force is more invisible but equally decisive: it is the threshold of activation. Some cats are born with a neurophysiological structure that makes them particularly reactive to stimulation—sounds, movements, contacts—while others maintain a quiet interior that makes them seem imperturbable. It is as if every cat were tuned in to its own perceptive frequency, a unique way of feeling the world. Breeds with high sensitivity and therefore a low threshold of activation are the Siamese, the Abyssinian, the Bengal, the Devon Rex—reactive, perceptive, emotionally intense—while the Maine Coon, the Siberian, and the Norwegian Forest Cat are curious but well-balanced. And lastly we have the British Shorthair, the Chartreux, the Persian, the Ragdoll: they are less reactive, calmer, and need more intense stimulation to become active.

Finally, the third force: the environment. The experiences lived during the first months of life leave deep impressions in adult behavior. The way in which a kitten is touched, heard, welcomed, or ignored, the abundance of stimulation to which it is exposed, the type of relationship tried: all this contributes to molding its way of being in the world and reacting.

And it is precisely from the intertwining of these three dimensions that the extraordinary variety of temperaments, which makes every cat a universe unto itself, is born. Also, within a same breed, infinite nuances are revealed: a vivid reflection of the meeting between what was already written and what life has been able to write.

Temperament is not a fixed and immutable trait, but a dynamic predisposition that modifies over time in response to the environment, the experiences, and the relation with human beings. It is the result of a continuous interaction between genetics, development, and context.

And in all this, there is also room for mystery. The cat—with its agile presence that does not hold us tight but accompanies us, and which in its own unique way shows us who we are and who we could become.

Ewa Princi

Cat and Witches

Anyone who has had the opportunity to meet a cat can certainly appreciate its fascination and mystery, but only those who have been fortunate enough to be *chosen* by a cat can understand the universe hidden behind the depth of its eyes.

Walking sinuously and silently at the edges of our world, the cat has accompanied humanity since the dawn of time.

Able hunter, it protected ancient populations from diseases carried by rodents, thereby becoming the go-between of divine benevolence.

The contact between the cat and the kingdom of the Gods is particularly clear in the ancient religions: from Ancient Egypt, where the goddess Bastet was depicted with a feline head and the body of a woman, to the cold lands of Northern Europe, where the Norse goddess Freyja usually traveled on a chariot drawn by majestic cats.

Stories and legends coming from every corner of the globe and the cat's natural propensity to move in obscurity contributed to increase its fame as guardian of mysteries inaccessible to human beings; and soon, in the collective imagination, the cat became a messenger capable of moving between the visible and the invisible worlds.

However, in 1233 a Papal Bull decreed that the cat, in particular the black one, represented an emanation of the devil, or an ally of his followers. So, the affable feline turned from an emissary of the gods into a deceptive spirit and accomplice of the force of evil.

Because of its independence and elusive nature, the cat was associated with feminine energies not subject to masculine dominion, and for this reason it appeared iconographically alongside the witches in the role of *familiaris*, a member of the family.

The *familiaris* was considered a magical assistant, often of a spiritual nature, whose task was to assist the witch in her practices and in her esoteric path, offering her protection and precious advice.

According to folklore and magic tradition, the cat was considered a precious ally thanks to its innate harmony with these subtle energies. Various European popular stories tell that the most powerful witches could change shape or "blend" with their own feline ally, acquiring the ability to see through its eyes.

The physical and temperamental peculiarities of the cat and the events that marked its history, feeding still today the thought that it has a deep bond with the slender veil that we call magic, accomplishes also its extraordinary sensitivity and its ability to reflect our anxieties, dissolving them with their purrs and enigmatic gaze.

Anyone who has had a cat and has been lucky enough to feel its warmth cuddled on one's heart, who has lost themselves in its eyes, knows that the term "domestic animal" cannot contain its true essence, for it is much more: it is an old soul that has chosen us from among millions of people.

Living with a cat allows us to learn something more about ourselves and the world around us every day.

Its calm mastery of indolence and the sudden spurts of joy remind us that life is not only a frantic pursuit, but a delicate balance that we must earn to be able to fully live our existence.

With innate wisdom and glances so profound that they seem to probe the soul, it invites us to raise our spirit toward unexplored horizons. It gives us the awareness that life is not only matter, but it vibrates with energy: it is up to us to sharpen our gaze.

The life of someone who has loved a cat is a rich life, because they have caressed a fragment of mystery, have hosted a whisper of magic in their heart, and have understood that we are not—and will never be—truly alone.

Federica Vanini

CATS *of* NATURE

Tied to the elements and the spirits of the earth, the Cats of Nature are ancient custodians of their connection with the natural world.

With their primordial instinct and imposing presence, they evoke the power of the trees, the rivers, and the wind. These cats recall the strength of the elements, root the soul, and protect those around it.
We have associated a flower or a magic plant with each of them, which reflects their traits, making them perfect companions for those living in harmony with the environment.

KURILIAN BOBTAIL

ORIGIN: Kuril Islands

DISTINCTIVE CHARACTERISTICS: Short, rolled-up tail, compact body, resistant fur

PERSONALITY: Loyal, observant, territorial

MAGICAL POWERS: Protects from negative external influences and establishes energy boundaries

ROLE IN MAGIC: Magical guardian, ideal in rituals of defense

Origin and History

Originating from the Kuril Islands, between Russia and Japan, the Kurilian Bobtail is an ancient breed, which developed naturally in the harsh climates of the archipelago that it freely populates still today. These cats were seen as a source of good fortune for fishermen, who kept them on the boats to keep rodents away.
Its short, rolled-up tail contributed to strengthening the image of this cat as symbol of uniqueness and protection.

Physical and Behavioral Characteristics

The Kurilian Bobtail has a muscular and compact body. The short tail serves to avoid excessive loss of body heat. It almost looks like a lynx because of the thick coat and the tufts of fur that come out of the ears. This cat is agile despite the solid build, curious, and an excellent hunter.

Magical Bond: Attributed Spiritual Qualities and Powers

The Kurilian Bobtail is considered a powerful protector of energy. Its presence helps create safe energy boundaries and averts the negative influences, just like the fern, a plant that is traditionally associated with the practices of protection. It is ideal for those practicing rituals of defense against hostile energies.

Relation with the Owner

The Kurilian Bobtail is perfect for creating a safe space during magic practices, keeping the concentration of the person accompanying it steady. Its capacity to perceive changes in energy makes it a vigilant custodian, always ready to defend its physical and spiritual territory.

I give you a secret, keep it in the wind

TURKISH ANGORA

ORIGIN: Türkiye

DISTINCTIVE CHARACTERISTICS: Long, silky fur; eyes of a variety of colors, even heterochromic; elegant body

PERSONALITY: Sensitive, affectionate, harmonious

MAGICAL POWERS: Favors energy flow and emotional lightness

ROLE IN MAGIC: Facilitates practices of relaxation and purification

Origin and History

The Turkish Angora is one of the most ancient feline breeds, and its name comes from the city of Ankara, in Türkiye, called Angora in the past. The story goes that Mohammad had a red Turkish Angora, whose fur turned as white as snow during a very harsh winter. Legend says that if you whisper a wish into the ear of this feline, it sends the wish up to the sky.

Physical and Behavioral Characteristics

The Turkish Angora has an elegant, slender body, with long silky fur, which can have various variants and colors.
It can have differently colored eyes, and with their almond shape they contribute to its magnetic and mysterious character.
It is an agile cat, with an affectionate and sociable nature.
It can develop a strong bond with its human companion, but it preserves an independence that makes it a lover of external spaces.

Magical Bond: Attributed Spiritual Qualities and Powers

Its presence is considered capable of dissolving emotional blocks and energy stagnation. It is viewed as a facilitator of transformation and adaptation, capable of bringing lightness and grace at times of difficulty. Its talents bestow calm and clarity, making it possible to face changes with confidence and serenity. For this reason it is associated with Chamomile, a soothing plant capable of dissolving tension.

Relation with the Owner

The Turkish Angora is tied to the element of the air, and is a precious ally in rituals of removal and transformation.
It is perfect for practices of release and cleansing, an important aid for dissolving negative energies and facilitating emotional flow.

Its sensitivity helps one perceive thin vibrations and immaterial presences, both natural and supernatural, and to reconnect with one's own inner essence.

FOCUS

A Cat Dear to Prophets and Heroes

OVER THE YEARS, VARIOUS LEGENDS HAVE EMERGED AROUND THE TURKISH ANGORA, TRAVELING FROM MOUTH TO MOUTH UNTIL THE PRESENT DAY. IN ONE, THE TURKISH ANGORA OF THE PROPHET MOHAMMAD, HAVING TURNED WHITE AFTER A PARTICULARLY COLD WINTER, LIKED TO SLEEP ON THE SLEEVE OF ITS OWNER.

HE WAS SO FOND OF THE FELINE THAT ONE DAY, NOT WANTING TO WAKE HIM, HE DECIDED TO CUT OFF THE SLEEVE OF THE GARMENT RATHER THAN DISTURB THE CAT.

ACCORDING TO ANOTHER LEGEND, THE NATIONAL TURKISH HERO MUSTAFA KEMAL ATATÜRK SUCCEEDED IN HIS QUEST TO FOUND THE TURKISH REPUBLIC, BECOMING THE FIRST PRESIDENT, BECAUSE HE WAS CHOSEN BY A TURKISH ANGORA WHO BIT HIS ANKLE, TRANSMITTING DIVINE FAVOR TO HIM.

IT IS SAID THAT THIS SAME ATATÜRK, WHO DIED IN 1938, WILL BE BORN AGAIN ONE DAY AS A TURKISH ANGORA WITH ONE GOLDEN EYE AND THE OTHER ONE BLUE.

LAPERM

ORIGIN: United States

DISTINCTIVE CHARACTERISTICS: Curly, light fur; bright eyes; original appearance

PERSONALITY: Affectionate, playful, sociable

MAGICAL POWERS: Clears emotional blocks, stimulates transformation

ROLE IN MAGIC: Emotional regulator, supports inner changes

Origin and History

The LaPerm is a relatively recent breed, born spontaneously in the United States in the 1980s. The first LaPerm was born on a farm in Oregon from a domestic cat kept outdoors.

In a litter of six kittens, one kitten had absolutely no fur, unlike its siblings. In the eighth week, the cat started to grow soft, curly fur, then passing this genetic characteristic on to its own kittens.

Physical and Behavioral Characteristics

The LaPerm has a medium-sized, slender, and muscular build. Its curly fur can be of various lengths and density. The eyes are large, often golden or green. It is an affectionate and sociable cat that seeks the proximity of its human companion, sometimes jumping into his lap of its own free will.

Magical Bond: Attributed Spiritual Qualities and Powers

It is believed that the presence of the LaPerm helps dissolve energy tension. Its energy stimulates creativity and helps overcome moments of emotional stress. It helps let the unnecessary go without remorse and facilitate the passage to new phases of life, like the Dog Rose, a flower used in the rituals of energy healing.

Relation with the Owner

The LaPerm is a companion that inspires trust in change.
Its capacity to adapt to situations and its affectionate nature make it a precious ally for those who need strength and resilience in moments of transformation. It is a perfect inspiration for those trying to change difficulties into new opportunities.

MAINE COON

ORIGIN: United States

DISTINCTIVE CHARACTERISTICS: Long, thick fur; large, muscular body; thick tail

PERSONALITY: Affectionate, protective, friendly

MAGICAL POWERS: Protects the house, amplifies the sense of grounding

ROLE IN MAGIC: Custodian of domestic equilibrium, helps in rituals of protection

Origin and History

The Maine Coon is one of the oldest feline breeds of North America, with origins intertwined between myth and reality. The story goes that the first one was born from a crossbreeding between a raccoon and a lynx, two animals well adapted to the harsh climates of Maine. Another legend says that it is descended from the cats of Marie Antoinette, transported to America during the French Revolution.

Physical and Behavioral Characteristics

With its impressive body, the Maine Coon is the largest domestic breed of cat. The long, thick fur is a shield against the cold, while the long, fluffy tail is reminiscent of a raccoon. The eyes, large and clear, convey a sense of curiosity and calm.
Despite its impressive dimensions, it is known for its sociable and affectionate nature, with a strong attachment to its human family. Protective and gentle, it is an ideal companion for those looking for a cat that loves children.

Magical Bond: Attributed Spiritual Qualities and Powers

The Maine Coon is often considered the custodian of domestic energies. Its connection with nature, its love for the outdoors, and its passion for water make it ideal for anyone practicing magic tied to the elements, in particular the earth. This cat amplifies a sense of stability, creating a balanced and serene environment, and absorbing the negative energies coming from the outside, as does salvia, a purifying plant par excellence.

Relation with the Owner

The Maine Coon is the ideal ally for strengthening intuition and determination during rituals, offering emotional stability and energy support. Its natural calm nature makes it the perfect companion for magic practices focused on maintaining domestic harmony. With its imposing but reassuring presence, the Maine Coon is much more than a simple cat: it is a custodian, a protector, and a symbol of balance.

FOCUS

Argus Filch and Mrs. Norris: The Eyes of Magic

IN THE WORLD OF "HARRY POTTER," MRS. NORRIS IS THE FAITHFUL AND EERIE CAT OF ARGUS FILCH, CARETAKER OF HOGWARTS. EVEN THOUGH IN THE BOOKS SHE IS DESCRIBED AS A THIN TABBY WITH BULGING EYES, IN THE MOVIES SHE IS PLAYED BY A MAINE COON, A PERFECT CHOICE BECAUSE OF ITS IMPOSING APPEARANCE AND PENETRATING GAZE.

MRS. NORRIS IS MORE THAN A SIMPLE CAT: SHE SEEMS TO HAVE A SUPERNATURAL CONNECTION WITH FILCH, APPEARING SUDDENLY AT THE MOST INCONVENIENT MOMENTS FOR THE STUDENTS. HER CAPACITY FOR PATROLLING THE CASTLE AND "REPORTING" EVEN THE SMALLEST INFRACTION MAKES HER AN ALMOST MAGICAL CREATURE.

IN MANY CULTURES, CATS ARE VIEWED AS GUARDIANS OF INVISIBLE BOUNDARIES, AND MRS. NORRIS PERFECTLY EMBODIES THIS ARCHETYPE, COMBINING THE MASSIVE PRESENCE OF THE MAINE COON WITH THE WORLD OF MAGIC OF WHICH SHE IS A PART.

SACRED CAT OF BURMA

ORIGIN: Burma (Myanmar)

DISTINCTIVE CHARACTERISTICS: Long, silky fur; intense blue eyes; dark tips and white paws

PERSONALITY: Calm, affectionate, devoted

MAGICAL POWERS: Harmonizes energies, promotes inner peace

ROLE IN MAGIC: Spiritual custodian, helps in meditation and rituals of equilibrium

Origin and History

According to legend, in the distant past many temples were built in Burma to honor the goddess Tsun Kyan-Kse. One day, some marauders entered the most important of these temples and killed the old guardian priest of the place. When his white cat prayed at the statue of the goddess to take the soul of the priest into the afterlife, its coat became golden and its eyes turned sapphire blue.
Only the paws remained white, as a symbol of purity.

Physical and Behavioral Characteristics

The semi-long and soft fur, the dark tips on the face, ears, and tail, and the white paws make it unmistakable. Its blue eyes convey all the sweetness typical of this breed. It is known for its devotion, which also leads it to follow its human companion around the house seeking affection.

Magical Bond: Attributed Spiritual Qualities and Powers

It is said that the presence of the Sacred Cat of Burma promotes inner peace, making it a perfect assistant for someone searching for serenity in their magical practices and meditation. This cat is a powerful harmonizer of energies like the Lotus Flower, symbol of purity and spiritual harmony.

Relation with the Owner

The Sacred Cat of Burma represents a spiritual ally that inspires mental clarity. Its capacity to harmonize the energies makes it indispensable for rituals of balance and purification. Its hypnotic gaze helps the human companion distance themselves from everyday worries, establishing an exclusive connection with their own mind.

NORWEGIAN FOREST CAT

ORIGIN: Scandinavia

DISTINCTIVE CHARACTERISTICS: Long, thick fur; green or golden eyes; sturdy build

PERSONALITY: Independent, explorer, affectionate

MAGICAL POWERS: Connection with the spirits of nature, protection of the energy boundaries

ROLE IN MAGIC: Reinforces the bond with the Earth, balances the natural energies, and protects during the rituals

Origin and History

Originating in Scandinavia, the Norwegian Forest Cat is tied to Norse mythology. The story goes that the goddess Freyja used a pair of these cats to pull her chariot. This sturdy breed, accustomed to harsh Nordic climates, was considered on a par with a guardian spirit of the forests. Many fairy tales of Nordic folklore have an enchanted cat called Skogkatt as protagonist.

Physical and Behavioral Characteristics

With its thick, water-repellent fur, the Norwegian Forest Cat is perfectly adapted to cold climates. One of its special features is the tufts of fur between the toes, that protect it from humidity and prevent it from sinking in the snow. The body is large and muscular, with sturdy legs and a long, thick tail.

The eyes are oval-shaped, often green or golden: they are colors that convey an intense connection with nature.

This cat is also described as a "gentle giant" with a mild nature but enterprising disposition.

Magical Bond: Attributed Spiritual Qualities and Powers

The Norwegian Forest Cat epitomizes the bond with elemental magic. Still today, in many Central European countries, popular folklore attributes to this breed a particular connection with atmospheric phenomena.

It is said that it is able to communicate with the entities of the woods and protect the energy boundaries of the home.

In tune with the fir tree, symbol of protection and connection with nature, this cat amplifies the perception of natural energies, making it ideal for those who work with spells tied to the Earth, fertility, and protection.

Relation with the Owner

This cat is a perfect companion for those looking for an ally in natural magic. It reinforces the bond with the elements and helps ground the energy during the rituals. Its calm but vigilant disposition offers emotional security and spiritual protection, making it a custodian.

FOCUS

From Freyja's Chariot to the Forest

IN NORSE MYTHOLOGY, FREYJA, GODDESS OF LOVE, FERTILITY, AND WAR, USED TO TRAVEL ACROSS THE SKIES ON A CHARIOT DRAWN BY TWO POWERFUL CATS, SYMBOLS OF STRENGTH AND PROTECTION. THE NORWEGIAN FOREST CAT, WITH ITS THICK COAT AND REGAL BEARING, EMBODIES PERFECTLY THE IMAGE OF THESE SACRED COMPANIONS. THEIR PRESENCE WAS SEEN AS A SOURCE OF GOOD FORTUNE, BELIEVED TO DRIVE AWAY NEGATIVE ENERGIES AND PROTECT THE FAMILY. IN NORTHERN COUNTRIES, TRADITION HELD THAT NEWLYWEDS, UPON ENTERING THEIR NEW HOME, HAD TO PREPARE A BOWL OF MILK FOR THE HOUSEHOLD CAT. IF THE CAT DRANK IT, IT MEANT THE HOUSE WAS INHABITED BY A GOOD SPIRIT.

LEGENDS TELL THAT FREYJA BROUGHT PROSPERITY TO THOSE WHO TREATED THEIR CATS WELL, A MESSAGE THAT IS REFLECTED IN THE MODERN CONCEPT OF THE NORWEGIAN FOREST CAT AS A SYMBOL OF HARMONY AND CONNECTION WITH NATURE.

SIBERIAN CAT

ORIGIN: Russia

DISTINCTIVE CHARACTERISTICS: Long, thick fur; sturdy build; green or golden eyes

PERSONALITY: Affectionate, independent, adaptable

MAGICAL POWERS: Stabilizes the energies, absorbs negativity

ROLE IN MAGIC: Domestic protector, promotes rooting and energy security

Origin and History

The Siberian is an ancient breed, tied to the wild lands and the harsh climates of the Russian taiga. The story goes that in the Middle Ages, it acted as custodian of the monasteries in Siberia, capable of facing snow and ice thanks to its extraordinary adaptability. Its capacity to orient itself and survive also in the most hostile landscapes has made it a symbol of strength and resistance.

Physical and Behavioral Characteristics

The Siberian has a sturdy, muscular body, with long and water-repellent fur that defends it from the freezing cold. It usually attaches itself to one member of the family that it is part of, and shows this connection by devoting particular attention to them.

Magical Bond: Attributed Spiritual Qualities and Powers

The Siberian is considered a custodian of the domestic environment, and an ally that offers security and strength, just like the support that the birch gives us in the realm of magic. Its connection with the earth and with the natural forces makes it perfect for anyone looking to connect their own inner and outer reality.

Relation with the Owner

The capacity of the Siberian to perceive the vibrations of the environment around it also allows the human accompanying it to identify and push away negative influences. Its reassuring presence is a firm support for every practice connected to the world of nature and awareness.

SOMALI CAT

ORIGIN: United States

DISTINCTIVE CHARACTERISTICS: Medium-long copper-colored fur; thick tail; intense eyes

PERSONALITY: Active, enthusiastic, fascinating

MAGICAL POWERS: Feeds passion, attracts opportunity

ROLE IN MAGIC: Enhances rituals of attractions and personal growth

Origin and History

The Somali is a breed that emerged in the 1960s, but its genetic origins date back to the ancient populations of African cats. It probably derives from some specimens of Abyssinian with long fur, which at the end of the 19th century were brought to the West.
Its lively nature, together with its long, reddish fur and the thick tail, have earned it the nickname of "fox cat."

Physical and Behavioral Characteristics

The Somali has a slender, muscular body, with fur characterized by warm nuances that evoke the color of sand or copper.
The eyes, large and almond-shaped, convey liveliness and curiosity with every glance. It is an extremely active and playful cat, which enjoys exploring and social interaction. Its agility and intelligence make it a natural hunter, always on the quest for new incentives and adventures with which to fill its days.

Magical Bond: Attributed Spiritual Qualities and Powers

The Somali is linked to the fire element. It stimulates action and self-confidence, and is capable of reawakening our vital energy like ginger root does in the world of plants. Its warm and enveloping energy acts like a flame that awakens inner strength, perfect for giving courage, motivation, and passion in the people near it.

Relation with the Owner

The Somali is the perfect ally in rituals that require channeling personal energy to manifest desires and intentions.
Its playful and curious nature helps the human companion overcome their fears and view the difficulties as opportunities of growth. Its presence instills warmth and dynamism, making it an ideal companion for those aiming to face life with passion and determination.
It is ideal for anyone following practices connected to the law of attraction and manifesting, since it amplifies the capacity to focus on the objectives and obtaining concrete results.

FOCUS

The Cat and the Woman: A Legendary Alliance

THE SOMALI IS A BREED THAT STRENGTHENS THE CHARACTER OF ITS HUMAN COMPANION, CONSTANTLY SEARCHING FOR KINDRED SPIRITS.

A SOMALI STORY TELLS OF THE PROFOUND BOND BETWEEN THE CAT AND THE WOMAN—ACCORDING TO THE LEGEND, THE ONLY PERSON WITH THE SAME STRENGTH OF CHARACTER AS THE CAT. THE LEGEND SAYS THAT WHEN THE WORLD WAS CREATED, THE CAT WAS A GREAT FRIEND OF THE ANTELOPE. ONE DAY, HOWEVER, THE ANTELOPE WAS TORN TO PIECES BY THE LION. THE CAT THOUGHT THAT THE LION WAS BETTER THAN THE ANTELOPE BECAUSE IT WAS STRONGER, SO IT DECIDED TO BECOME THE LION'S FRIEND. THE LION, HOWEVER, WAS CRUSHED BY A HERD OF ELEPHANTS. WHEN THE CAT WANTED TO BECOME THE ELEPHANTS' FRIEND, IT SAW A MAN KILL AN ELEPHANT. SO IT DECIDED TO BECOME THE MAN'S FRIEND.

BUT WHEN, DURING A FIGHT, THE MAN WAS HIT BY HIS WIFE, THE CAT DECIDED THAT THE WOMAN WAS THE ONLY CREATURE WORTHY OF ITS FRIENDSHIP, BECAUSE HER STRENGTH HAD BEATEN EVERY OTHER ANIMAL.

ABYSSINIAN CAT

ORIGIN: Ethiopia

DISTINCTIVE CHARACTERISTICS: Short, nuanced fur; almond-shaped eyes; slender body

PERSONALITY: Lively, curious, enterprising

MAGICAL POWERS: Brings solar energy and mental clarity

ROLE IN MAGIC: Activator of vitality, useful in the rituals of manifestation

Origin and History

The Abyssinian is one of the oldest feline breeds. Recent studies mention origins connected to Southeast Asia, even if the name suggests a connection with Ethiopia (at one time called Abyssinia). The story goes that in ancient times these cats were considered to be the bearers of light and spiritual strength, capable of leading the souls in the kingdom of the afterworld. This connection with the light has made the Abyssinian a symbol of fertility and renewal.

Physical and Behavioral Characteristics

The Abyssinian is an elegant cat, with an agile and slender body. The short fur is typically nuanced, and the almond-shaped eyes convey a lively intelligence. It is a cat with an explorer's nature, but deeply affectionate and loyal to its human companion.

Magical Bond: Attributed Spiritual Qualities and Powers

The Abyssinian is connected to solar energy and inner strength. It helps dissipate stagnant energies and to bring clarity in moments of confusion, like the Sunflower, a flower symbolically the bearer of vitality. Its presence inspires strength of will and determination, essential for those practicing the magic of renewal and manifestation.

Relation with the Owner

The Abyssinian is a companion that brings decisiveness and motivation. It is the ideal ally to encourage the search for new opportunities. Its curious and dynamic nature stimulates courage and the desire to let the energies of the past flow, helping overcome emotional and spiritual blocks.

SPIRITUAL CATS

Silent custodians of the invisible world, the Spiritual Cats amplify intuition and perception.

Its ethereal presence and gaze that seems to go through the veils of reality guide toward inner awareness and the connection with subtler energies. These cats are precious allies for those who follow a spiritual path, meditate, dream, or desire to learn to interpret the language of the invisible. To each of them we have associated two different chakras, which reflect the traits of every cat; the support of this can lead to the discovery of the deep self.

DONSKOY CAT

ORIGIN: Russia

DISTINCTIVE CHARACTERISTICS: Hairless; elastic and rough skin; large ears

PERSONALITY: Intuitive, affectionate, enigmatic

MAGICAL POWERS: Removes the veils of the unconscious, promotes inner regeneration

ROLE IN MAGIC: Deep healer, connected to the lunar rituals

Origin and History

The Donskoy is a Russian breed that spontaneously appeared in 1987 at Rostov on the Don. Unlike the Canadian Sphynx, the Donskoy (also called Don Sphynx) has its own genetic mutation, which is responsible for its lack of fur. It is considered a mysterious and fascinating cat, as well as a symbol of resilience and change. It tends to be associated with the occult due to its mysterious appearance and its penetrating, almost human gaze.

Physical and Behavioral Characteristics

The Donskoy has a bare, warm skin and slender body. It has broad ears and slanted eyes. The tail is large at the base but tapers toward the tip. It is an affectionate and meek cat, sensitive to emotional changes and very curious.

Magical Bond: Attributed Spiritual Qualities and Powers

The Donskoy is associated with the liberation of blocked energies and psychic regeneration, traits that are bound peripherally to the seventh chakra. Its presence helps let go of what has been overcome, and transforms wounds in awareness. It is a good ally to face periods of profound personal and spiritual transformation.

Relation with the Owner

The Donskoy is a perfect companion for those working with the magic of the shadows, dreams, and lunar cycles. Its energy accompanies it in the voyage through the hidden parts of the soul, offering a silent but constant guide toward rebirth. Its inner strength embodies the personal power and the determination expressed by the third chakra.

RUSSIAN BLUE

ORIGIN: Russia

DISTINCTIVE CHARACTERISTICS: Short blue-gray coat with silver reflections; emerald green eyes; elegant, muscular build.

PERSONALITY: Calm, adaptable, discreet

MAGICAL POWERS: Bearer of serenity, promotes intuition and psychic sensitivity

ROLE IN MAGIC: Meditative guide, facilitates extrasensory perception

Origin and History

The Russian Blue is a feline breed with origins shrouded in mystery. It is believed that it comes from the port city of Arkhangelsk, in northwest Russia, where it was known as "Cat of Arkhangelsk." The breed was introduced into Europe in the 19th century, rapidly earning popularity due to its beauty and distinctive nature. The story goes that these cats were appreciated at the courts of the Russian Tsars and European sovereigns.

Physical and Behavioral Characteristics

The Russian Blue is a medium-sized cat with an elegant, muscular body. Its coat is blue-gray with silvery reflections, while the eyes, of an intense green, give its gaze an intense and penetrating expression.

It tends to become deeply attached to one person, yet it never demands attention. It is naturally drawn to a human companion with a calm temperament—much like its own.

Magical Bond: Attributed Spiritual Qualities and Powers

The Russian Blue is seen as a bearer of serenity for its chosen human. Its presence is considered capable of amplifying intuition and psychic sensitivity, promoting the perception of the potential beyond the form. Its calm aura, linked to the first chakra, fosters a sense of safety and makes it an ideal companion during the process of introspection.

Relation with the Owner

For anyone practicing the magic arts, the Russian Blue serves as meditative guide, promoting the perception of thoughts and sensations. Its empathetic nature allows it to tune in to the emotions of the owner, offering emotional stability during the spiritual journeys. In addition, it represents a silent support during the magic processes that require a strong expenditure of energy, promoting an environment of peace and concentration, and stimulating the awareness linked to the sixth chakra.

FOCUS

A Cat at the Court of the Tsars

AS EARLY AS THE MID-19TH CENTURY, THE RUSSIAN BLUE FOUND ITS PLACE AT COURT. DUE TO ITS PARTICULAR COLOR AND ELEGANT BEARING, IT WAS THE PREFERRED PET OF THE NOBILITY, FROM THE GRAND DUKES TO THE TSARS THEMSELVES.

A LEGEND SAYS THAT, CONSIDERING THESE FELINES A SYMBOL OF HAPPINESS, AT COURT THEY WERE PLACED IN THE BEDROOMS OF THE CHILDREN TO PROTECT THEM FROM THE EVIL SPIRITS WHICH COULD INFEST THE WALLS. ONE RUSSIAN SOVEREIGN WELL KNOWN FOR HIS UNCONDITIONAL LOVE OF THIS BREED WAS TSAR PETER I. TOGETHER WITH HIS DAUGHTER ELIZABETH, HE STARTED TO RAISE THEM HIMSELF, ALLOWING THEM TO ROAM UNDISTURBED THROUGH THEIR PRIVATE ROOMS. FOR TSARINA CATHERINE II, THE RUSSIAN BLUE WAS THE IDEAL TRIBUTE TO GIVE TO FOREIGN AMBASSADORS. ONE OF THESE FELINES EVEN MADE IT TO QUEEN VICTORIA OF THE UNITED KINGDOM, ADDING TO HER ALREADY-LARGE COLLECTION OF CATS.

SPHYNX CAT

ORIGIN: Canada

DISTINCTIVE CHARACTERISTICS: Lack of fur; warm skin; large, hypnotic eyes

PERSONALITY: Affectionate, sensitive, curious

MAGICAL POWERS: Reveals the truth, amplifies internal perception

ROLE IN MAGIC: Spiritual guide, ideal for introspection and rituals of truth

Origin and History

The Sphynx is a recent breed which emerged in New Mexico in the 19th century from a spontaneous genetic mutation that caused its lack of fur. The attempts of actual selective breeding began in Canada in the 1970s. The nakedness of the Sphynx is often viewed as a symbol of truth, vulnerability, and deep connection with what lies beyond the material world.

Physical and Behavioral Characteristics

The Sphynx has a slim, muscular body, large ears, and magnetic eyes. Despite the alien appearance, it is extremely affectionate, curious, and lively. It loves physical contact and often snuggles close to find warmth. Unlike many feline species, it is not wary of other domestic animals.

Magical Bond: Attributed Spiritual Qualities and Powers

The Sphynx is associated with the revelation of the most authentic self. It is perfect for moments of spiritual transformation, offering support and total presence. Its nakedness and the need for physical contact resonate with intuitive understanding of who we are, linked to the third chakra.

Relation with the Owner

The Sphynx is a slender and sensitive guide, capable of accompanying one during inner journeys and in the most intimate spiritual practices. This support for spiritual openness is linked to the seventh chakra and encourages connection with the higher self. In addition, the Sphynx is ideal for deep meditation and psychic perception practices.

DEVON REX

ORIGIN: United Kingdom

DISTINCTIVE CHARACTERISTICS: Short, wavy fur; very large ears; triangular face

PERSONALITY: Affectionate, playful, very intelligent

MAGICAL POWERS: Stimulates empathetic connection; brings lightness and inspiration

ROLE IN MAGIC: Useful ally in dreamlike rituals and emotional intuition

Origin and History

The Devon Rex was born in 1960 in Devonshire, England, from a case of spontaneous mutation similar to that of the Cornish Rex.
The first specimen, Kirlee, was born from the union of a domestic cat and a stray cat and showed unique traits: wavy fur, short face, and enormous ears.
This cat was soon recognized for its extraordinary intelligence, and is often compared to an elf because of its fairy-tale appearance.

Physical and Behavioral Characteristics

The Devon Rex is slender but strong and agile, and loves to climb. Its fur is fine, wavy, or curly, very velvety to the touch. The enormous ears and large eyes give it a constantly curious expression. It is a very affectionate cat, often called "velcro-cat" for its tendency to always stay close to its human companion. It does not like being excluded from family activities.

Magical Bond: Attributed Spiritual Qualities and Powers

The Devon Rex brings inspiration and empathetic connection. Its lightness helps release mental tension, making it a perfect ally for those who seek deeper states of awareness beyond consciousness. It is considered an energetic messenger: it helps perceive the emotions of others, leading to intuitions that emerge through the heart more than through the mind. This desire for emotional connection resonates with the energy linked to the second chakra, associated with the management of emotions.

Relation with the Owner

The Devon Rex is a companion that helps the owner open up to a deep emotional dimension and empathetic intuition. It is ideal for rituals connected to nonverbal communication and the interpretation of dreams.
Its presence plays with the subtlest energies, influencing the spiritual well-being of its human companion.
Its need for interaction expresses the energy of authentic communication linked to the fifth chakra. Also for this reason it is an excellent support during moments of emotional tiredness, channeling light and lightness.

FOCUS

The Elfin Feline of Devonshire

THE DEVON REX HAS RATHER PECULIAR PHYSICAL CHARACTERISTICS, SUCH AS LARGE EYES AND WIDE EARS, THAT MAKE IT LOOK A LOT LIKE AN ELF.
BUT IT IS NOT ONLY THE APPEARANCE THAT THIS CAT AND THE FAIRY CREATURE HAVE IN COMMON.
ACCORDING TO ANGLO-SAXON MYTHOLOGY, SOME FAIRY CREATURES SIMILAR TO ELVES, KNOWN AS PIXIES, LIVE IN DEVONSHIRE, A REGION IN THE NORTH OF CORNWALL. DESCRIBED AS LITTLE FRIENDLY BEINGS, PIXIES ALSO LOVE LITTLE TRICKS, INCLUDING MAKING WANDERERS LOSE THEIR WAY. IN THE CITY OF OTTERY ST. MARY, IN EAST DEVON, PIXIE DAYS ARE STILL ORGANIZED TODAY, IN MEMORY OF THE DAY WHEN, AFTER HAVING ALMOST LED SOME MONKS TO THEIR DEATHS WITH ONE OF THEIR MISLEADING SPELLS, THESE CREATURES WERE KICKED OUT OF THE CITY FOREVER.

CORNISH REX

ORIGIN: United Kingdom

DISTINCTIVE CHARACTERISTICS: Very short, curly fur; slender body; large ears

PERSONALITY: Lively, curious, intelligent

MAGICAL POWERS: Stimulates the intuitive mind, dissolves mental blocks

ROLE IN MAGIC: Psychic catalyst, perfect for rituals of mental clarity

Origin and History

The Cornish Rex was born in 1950 in Cornwall, from a natural genetic mutation in a litter of domestic cats.
The first specimen, Kallibunker, had a short, curly coat, never seen before. This peculiarity immediately attracted attention, and the breed was selected for its physical uniqueness.

Physical and Behavioral Characteristics

The Cornish Rex has a long, slender, and muscular body, covered by a very short and wavy fur. Its ears are very large compared to the head, and the expressive eyes reveal an active intelligence.
It is a breed that has maintained the original nature of a farm cat—very curious and in continuous need of stimulation.

Magical Bond: Attributed Spiritual Qualities and Powers

The energy of the Cornish Rex is subtle but intense: it stimulates inner perception and dissolves mental blocks that prevent a clear and constant flow of thoughts. Its liveliness and curiosity reflect the spontaneity linked to the third chakra.

Relation with the Owner

The Cornish Rex helps its human companion open their mind and get in tune with their deep thoughts and intuitions. It is ideal, during practices of meditation, to receive inspiration from higher levels, and a useful ally for those practicing divination. It helps its human companions free themselves from the superfluous and to access a state of clear awareness closely linked to the seventh chakra—of consciousness and bliss.

GOOD BYE
1234567890
NOPQRSTUVWXYZ
ABCDEFGHIJKLM
YES
OUIJA
MYSTIFYING ORACLE
NO

SIAMESE CAT

ORIGIN: Thailand

DISTINCTIVE CHARACTERISTICS: Intense blue eyes; dark tips on light fur

PERSONALITY: Communicative, loyal, affectionate

MAGICAL POWERS: Increases intuition, fosters spiritual connection

ROLE IN MAGIC: Reinforces inner listening, protects during introspection, and supports the rituals of divination

Origin and History

Native of Thailand—historically known as Siam—the Siamese was venerated in Buddhist temples as a sacred cat. Reserved for members of the royal family, it was considered a spiritual guardian and symbol of protection. In fact, it was believed that a Siamese would welcome people's souls once they reached the world of the dead.

These legends consolidated its status as a bridge between the earthly world and the spiritual one.

Physical and Behavioral Characteristics

The elegant, slender, and muscular body of the Siamese conveys grace and strength. The fur is short and silky, while the blue eyes, deep and hypnotic, draw attention. It is known for its communicative nature, and is often described as a chatterbox—speaking to its human companion through sounds that convey emotion. Its need for attention, paired with a deep capacity for listening, makes it a unique companion, capable of forming intense bonds.

Magical Bond: Attributed Spiritual Qualities and Powers

The Siamese is a natural amplifier of intuition and subtle perception, characteristics that link it to the sixth chakra, associated with spiritual knowledge. Its energetic sensitivity allows it to perceive subtle changes in the surrounding environment and sense presences not perceptible to human eyes and ears. For this reason, it is believed to be a type of cat ideal for meditation and divination. Its eyes seem to penetrate the veil between the worlds, offering protection during processes of introspection.

Relation with the Owner

Next to its human companion, the Siamese strengthens the connection with supernatural presences, improving inner listening.

It is not only a custodian, but also a precious guide, capable of increasing emotional security and a sense of belonging.

Its vocal expression reflects the energy of the fifth chakra, linked to communication, and supports the free flow of ideas and opinions.

FOCUS

The Siamese and the Supernatural: The Cat of the Mystics

IN LITERATURE AND POPULAR CULTURE, THE SIAMESE IS OFTEN REPRESENTED BY A CAT CONNECTED TO THE SUPERNATURAL. IN THE FAMOUS SERIES OF CRIME NOVELS "THE CAT WHO . . ." BY LILIAN JACKSON BRAUN, THE SIAMESE CATS KOKO AND YUM YUM SUPPORT THE JOURNALIST JIM QWILLERAN IN SOLVING MYSTERIES, THANKS TO THEIR ALMOST SUPERNATURAL PERCEPTION. KOKO, IN PARTICULAR, SEEMS TO HAVE AN INFALLIBLE INSTINCT TO DISCOVER HIDDEN CLUES, AS IF IT COULD SEE BEYOND THE VISIBLE REALITY. THIS PRESUMED CONNECTION BETWEEN THE SIAMESE AND THE OCCULT IS REINFORCED BY ITS HYPNOTIC ELEGANCE AND ITS EXTRAORDINARY INTELLIGENCE. ALWAYS BELIEVED TO BE A BRIDGE BETWEEN THE PHYSICAL WORLD AND THE SPIRITUAL ONE, THE SIAMESE IS PERFECT FOR THOSE LOOKING FOR AN INTUITIVE GUIDE.

ORIENTAL CAT
(SHORTHAIR AND LONGHAIR)

ORIGIN: United States

DISTINCTIVE CHARACTERISTICS: Long-limbed body; light-colored eyes; wide variety of colors and coats

PERSONALITY: Expressive, sensitive, intense

MAGICAL POWERS: Channels the energy of the heart, amplifies nonverbal communication

ROLE IN MAGIC: Bridge between emotion and thought, useful in rituals of emotional awareness

Origin and History

The genetic roots of the Oriental can be found in Thailand, but the breed was developed in the United States in the 1970s as a genetic extension of the Siamese. Two variants exist: Shorthair (with short fur) and Longhair (with long, silky fur).
It is appreciated for its refined spirit and its capacity of "talking" with its gaze and body—so much so that it is seen as a cat with subtle and deep communication.

Physical and Behavioral Characteristics

Its body is elegant, slender and muscular, with large ears and almond-shaped eyes. It is one of the most communicative cats: it uses its body and gaze to express thoughts and emotions. It is also a very greedy cat and tends to get fat.

Magical Bond: Attributed Spiritual Qualities and Powers

The Oriental is a channel open between heart and mind. It stimulates the authentic expression of ourselves, a trait linked to the fifth chakra, with which communication is associated. Its energy helps find the correct language to communicate deep truths.

Relation with the Owner

The presence of the Oriental helps read what is moving inside us with clarity: its acute perception stimulates intuition, linked to the sixth chakra, the balance of which fosters a serene mind. It is perfect in rituals that require balance between thought and emotion, as it facilitates deep listening. It knows how to “speak without words”; this characteristic makes it ideal for awareness practices.

SINGAPURA CAT

ORIGIN: Singapore
(breed officially recognized in the United States)

DISTINCTIVE CHARACTERISTICS: Small size; short sepia-colored fur; large, luminous eyes

PERSONALITY: Gentle, attentive, energetic

MAGICAL POWERS: Enhances the connection with the inner child, stimulates gentleness and joy

ROLE IN MAGIC: Awakens the daily magic, ideal for rituals of gratitude

Origin and History

The Singapura is one of the smallest breeds in the world. It is believed that it descends from stray cats of Singapore, subsequently imported and recognized in the United States in the 1970s.
Its delicate appearance, small size, and lively energy have led to their being given many nicknames more or less connected to these physical characteristics, such as "zipper cat" or "love cat."

Physical and Behavioral Characteristics

The Singapura has a minute but muscular body, a light sepia-colored (ticked tabby) fur, large ears, large oval eyes (green, golden, or copper-colored), and a lively, gentle expression. Initially shy around strangers, after becoming acclimated it is curious, playful, and very affectionate. Despite its small size, it has great energy and loves to interact with the environment and people. It is very close to its human companion and needs to be around other cats.

Magical Bond: Attributed Spiritual Qualities and Powers

The Singapura is connected to the magic of simplicity and awareness. It brings lightness and heals our inner child, that part of us that preserves wonder and spontaneity. It encourages attention on the present and the beauty hidden in routine.
Its capacity to create deep bonds resonates with the energy of love and compassion linked to the fourth chakra.

Relation with the Owner

The Singapura is a gentle, sunny ally. It helps its human companion find pleasure again in the small things and connect with the most authentic and vulnerable part of themselves.
It is perfect for simple but profound rituals, centered on joy, gratitude, and emotional protection.
Its reassuring energy and the connection with the surrounding environment offer stability and security, two traits that stimulate the balance of the first chakra.

FOCUS

Fighting for Survival on the Streets of Singapore

EVEN IF TODAY IT IS KNOWN AS "ZIPPER CAT" BECAUSE OF ITS SMALL SIZE, ACCORDING TO SOME PEOPLE THIS CAT ORIGINATES IN THE STREETS AND DRAINPIPES OF SINGAPORE. AT ONE TIME IT WAS BELIEVED TO BE A RATHER ANNOYING STRAY, WHICH WAS THE REASON WHY THE LOCAL AUTHORITIES HUNTED IT AROUND THE CITY. THE ONLY WAY TO SAVE ITSELF FROM THE PERSECUTORS WAS THE SEWAGE PIPES, THE ACCESS TO WHICH WAS TOO NARROW FOR HUMANS. FROM THERE, IT EARNED THE SAD NICKNAME "DRAIN CAT," WHICH SOON DISAPPEARED ONCE THE BREED BECAME OF GREAT INTEREST FOR CAT LOVERS OF THE 1970S AND LATER—A LOVELY EVOLUTION FOR THIS MINUSCULE CAT WITH SUCH AN AFFECTIONATE GAZE!

TONKINESE CAT

ORIGIN: Canada, United States

DISTINCTIVE CHARACTERISTICS: Short, silky fur; aquamarine eyes; well-proportioned body

PERSONALITY: Joyful, affectionate, sociable

MAGICAL POWERS: Favors balance between light and shadow; harmonizes mixed emotions

ROLE IN MAGIC: Energetic mediator, ideal for rites of passage and rituals of inner reconciliation

Origin and History

The Tonkinese was born from the union between the Siamese and the Burmese, combining the best of both breeds. Even though various crossbreeding experiments had already been known since the 1930s, the breed was developed and formally recognized between the 1960s and 1970s in North America. It is known for its harmonious appearance, joyful nature, and great physical energy.

Physical and Behavioral Characteristics

The Tonkinese has an elegant but compact, muscular, and well-proportioned body. The fur is short and silky. The eyes, usually aquamarine or blue-green, have a hypnotic depth. It is a very sociable and talkative cat, known for its emotional intelligence.

Magical Bond: Attributed Spiritual Qualities and Powers

The Tonkinese is the mediator between contrasting elements inside and around us. It brings harmony where there are inner tensions, a trait that reflects the emotional balance governed by the fourth chakra. Its energy favors the integration of inner parts that fight, stimulating a unified view of the soul.

Relation with the Owner

The Tonkinese teaches the art of coexistence between opposites, a trait linked to the second chakra. It helps in rituals of personal and relationship reconciliation, supporting processes of transformation that start from acceptance. It is perfect for those working with practices of energy balance, healing of relationships, or resolution of inner conflicts.

BALINESE CAT

ORIGIN: United States

DISTINCTIVE CHARACTERISTICS: Medium-long, silky fur; blue eyes; elegant build

PERSONALITY: Active, talkative, affectionate

MAGICAL POWERS: Amplifies intuitive perception, stimulates emotional clarity

ROLE IN MAGIC: Energy channel, useful for practices of connection with the divine

Origin and History

The Balinese was born in the United States in the 1950s as a longhaired variant of the Siamese. Despite its exotic name, it has nothing to do with Bali.

The name was selected to evoke the fluid elegance of Balinese dancers, referring to the graceful bearing of these cats. It is often seen as a feline energy channel, thanks to its ethereal appearance and communicative nature.

Physical and Behavioral Characteristics

The Balinese has a slender and muscular body, very similar to the Siamese, but with a silky medium-length coat that flutters gently when it moves. Its luminous blue eyes reflect an extraordinary intelligence. It is an extremely talkative and active cat, needs constant stimulation, and prefers games of intelligence. It loves constant interaction and tends to be dominant toward other domestic animals.

Magical Bond: Attributed Spiritual Qualities and Powers

The Balinese is seen as an amplifier of intuition and deep bonds tied to feelings of love and compassion linked to the fourth chakra. Its presence favors clarity of feelings and perception of inner dynamics. For this reason, it is useful in moments of introspection, on paths of emotional healing, and during phases of spiritual openness: it is a living reflection of the soul.

Relation with the Owner

For a witch, the Balinese is a perfect companion during rituals of deep connection—both with the invisible world and the inner self—reflecting the spiritual energy of the seventh chakra. It is ideal for those working on practices of visualization and channeling of universal energy, as it increases awareness.

FOCUS

Balinese Dancers and the Sacred Power of Movement

WHILE NOT HAVING DIRECT TIES TO BALI, THE NAME "BALINESE" WAS CHOSEN FOR THIS CAT IN HONOR OF THOSE WHO PERFORM THIS TYPE OF DANCE, WITH ALMOST DIVINE GRACE AND LIGHTNESS.

IN PARTICULAR, THE BARONG DANCE IS ONE OF THE MOST INCREDIBLE TRADITIONAL SPECTACLES OF BALI, INVOLVING AND FASCINATING THE PUBLIC WITH ITS CHOREOGRAPHY AND COSTUMES. THE ETERNAL FIGHT BETWEEN GOOD AND EVIL IS BROUGHT TO THE STAGE, INSPIRED BY AN EPISODE OF THE "MAHABHARATA," ONE OF THE GREATEST HINDU EPIC POEMS.

IN THE DANCE, GOOD IS REPRESENTED BY BARONG, A GOD-ANIMAL WITH FOUR LEGS, SYMBOL OF FERTILITY, WHILE EVIL IS EMBODIED BY RANGDA, A WITCH. AT THE CONCLUSION OF THE FIGHT, WHICH DEPICTS AN ACTUAL FUSION OF DANCE AND THEATRICAL PERFORMANCE, BARONG DEFEATS RANGDA, BRINGING BALANCE BACK ON EARTH AND IN THE SKY.

PROTECTIVE CATS

With their attentive gaze and reassuring presence, Protective Cats safeguard the energy of the house and the people who live in it, bringing stability, calm, and comfort in moments of vulnerability.

To each of them we have associated magical crystals and stones, thinking about how each of these cats could amplify a specific protective vibration, purify the spaces, and harmonize the emotions. Silent guardians of the visible and invisible boundaries, they are ideal companions for those seeking a constant, deep, and reliable presence in their magic practice.

RAGDOLL

ORIGIN: United States

DISTINCTIVE CHARACTERISTICS: Semi-long, silky fur; blue eyes; gentle disposition

PERSONALITY: Gentle, relaxed, affectionate

MAGICAL POWERS: Brings peace and confidence, absorbs emotional tension, and creates harmony

ROLE IN MAGIC: Companion of healing, ideal for rituals of comfort and energy integration

Origin and History

The Ragdoll was selected in the 1960s in California by Ann Baker, who interbred domestic longhair cats to obtain a docile and affectionate breed. The name "Ragdoll" refers to the cat's tendency to relax completely when picked up. It is often associated with the energy of unconditional love and deep relaxation, and with a presence of a calming effect in the house.

Physical and Behavioral Characteristics

The Ragdoll is a cat with a muscular body and long, silky fur. It loves being picked up, and it gracefully accepts company without being intrusive. It is also patient and suitable for those who need a protective but reassuring energy. If desired, it can be trained to fetch.

Magical Bond: Attributed Spiritual Qualities and Powers

The Ragdoll is a channeler of harmony and inner peace. It is perfect for accompanying practices of emotional healing and energy recovery. It has a stable and engaging energy, which helps relieve tensions and anxieties.

Relation with the Owner

The Ragdoll is a precious ally in the practices of compassion and re-balancing. Combining its presence with the action of the amethyst, it is an ideal ally at times of emotional fatigue, and it supports one during relaxation practices, ritual work with the dream realm, and rituals of healing. Its calm energy protects gently, creating a soft space where the heart can rest.

CHARTREUX

ORIGIN: Türkiye, Iran

DISTINCTIVE CHARACTERISTICS: Short, blue-gray fur; copper or gold-colored eyes; sturdy build

PERSONALITY: Silent, loyal, thoughtful

MAGICAL POWERS: Mental calm, emotional protection, pushes away intrusive energies

ROLE IN MAGIC: Discreet sentry, ideal for rituals of introspection and stability

Origin and History

The Chartreux is an ancient breed, probably introduced in France by the crusaders of the Middle Ages. The story goes that they gave these cats to the monks because of their quiet and contemplative nature, as a reward for the hospitality in their monasteries. Thanks to its subdued meowing, it was believed to be a companion during silent meditation. It is associated with wisdom and the ability to see beyond the visual—a cat that observes and safeguards.

Physical and Behavioral Characteristics

The Chartreux has a compact body with a dense fur, soft and waterproof, always blue-gray. Its eyes, round and copper or gold-colored, hold a calm but deep gaze.
It is a reserved but very affectionate cat that establishes solid and long-lasting bonds. It loves calm and routine, moves with silent grace, and has a very developed capacity for adaptation.

Magical Bond: Attributed Spiritual Qualities and Powers

The Chartreux is a powerful emotional balancer. It helps calm the mind, strengthen the energy boundaries, and push away negative energies. It is ideal for those wanting to find serenity again, as well as internal protection. Its discreet but authoritative presence acts as a slender and constant barrier, maintaining the energy field clear and rooted. Its powers are intensified by obsidian, which contributes to forming a barrier against intrusive energies and helps introspection.

Relation with the Owner

For a witch, the Chartreux is a silent and vigilant ally. It accompanies the practices of meditation, reflection, and daily protection. It is ideal for those working with the mind or with rituals that require concentration and inner cleansing. It does not interfere, but observes and protects, like a guardian that operates at the subtler level.

FOCUS

The Blue Cat of the Monks

ACCORDING TO LEGEND, IT WAS THE KNIGHTS TEMPLAR WHO BROUGHT TO FRANCE THE FIRST CATS WITH THE BLUE-GRAY COAT AFTER THE CRUSADES, FINDING REFUGE IN THE CARTHUSIAN MONASTERIES. SILENT, INDEPENDENT, AND LETHAL FOR MICE, THESE FELINES QUICKLY BECAME THE IDEAL COMPANIONS FOR CONTEMPLATIVE LIFE.

IN THE MONASTERIES LIKE THE GRANDE CHARTREUSE—THE MOTHER HOUSE OF THE ORDER OF CARTHUSIANS—THE CATS WERE FREE TO MOVE AROUND THE CELLS, LOVED FOR THEIR CALM AND DISCREET NATURE.

IN REALITY, THE BOND WITH THE ORDER IS MORE LEGENDARY THAN DOCUMENTED, BUT THE VERY NAME OF THE BREED (*CHARTREUX* IN FRENCH, WHICH MEANS CARTHUSIAN) HAS RETAINED THIS SPIRITUAL ECHO.

OVER THE CENTURIES, THESE CATS BECAME KNOWN ALSO FOR THEIR THICK FUR, PRIZED ENOUGH TO BE USED IN THE MAKING OF CLOAKS. THE MODERN CHARTREUX, SELECTED IN THE 1930S BY THE LÉGER SISTERS, IS A DIRECT DESCENDANT OF THE ANCIENT MONASTIC PRESENCE.

EXOTIC SHORTHAIR

ORIGIN: United States

DISTINCTIVE CHARACTERISTICS: Short, soft, and dense fur; flat face; large eyes

PERSONALITY: Placid, affectionate, contemplative

MAGICAL POWERS: Calms the environment, stabilizes unstable emotions

ROLE IN MAGIC: Pacific custodian, ideal for rituals of quiet, harmony, and presence

Origin and History

The Exotic Shorthair was born in the United States in the 1960s, from the crossbreeding between a Persian and an American Shorthair. The objective of the breeders was to maintain the sweet appearance and the calm nature of the Persian, but with a coat easier to take care of. For this reason it was nicknamed "the lazy man's Persian". It is loved for its serene temperament and its affectionate discretion. Its presence is reassuring, stable, and often associated with silent protection.

Physical and Behavioral Characteristics

The Exotic Shorthair has a compact body, short legs, and large, round eyes. The fur is very thick, so much so that it seems like a plush fur coat. It is a calm cat that loves being around humans but does not impose its presence. It is the typical cat that transmits serenity just with its presence.

Magical Bond: Attributed Spiritual Qualities and Powers

The Exotic Shorthair is perfect for those looking for a calm presence by their side. In the realm of magic, it is ideal for maintaining a protected energy space, particularly during meditations of psycho-emotional recovery. Its powers are strengthened by selenite, a stone that permits an easier connection with the higher energies.

Relation with the Owner

The Exotic Shorthair is a companion that does not ask for anything, but gives a lot. It is ideal when working with subtle energies and is useful for staying centered and maintaining stability. Its contemplative nature makes it perfect for accompanying moments of connection with the inner self.

SCOTTISH FOLD

ORIGIN: Scotland

DISTINCTIVE CHARACTERISTICS: Ears folded forward, roundish body, large eyes

PERSONALITY: Composed, sensitive, reserved

MAGICAL POWERS: Harmonizes the spaces, re-balances the family energies

ROLE IN MAGIC: Domestic custodian, perfect for rituals of protection of the home and the community

Origin and History

The Scottish Fold is a Scottish breed that was born in the 1960s from a natural genetic mutation, which gave rise to its characteristic folded ears. The first cat with this distinctive feature was named Susie, and her unique appearance soon captivated breeders and cat lovers. In addition to the sweet, quiet appearance, this breed has always been associated with the protection of living spaces.

It is said that it brings balance in families and is particularly sensitive to environmental tension.

Physical and Behavioral Characteristics

The Scottish Fold has a roundish body with short legs, full face, and big, round eyes that convey a tender and placid expression. Its most distinctive trait are the ears folded forward, which give it a gentle air. It is a calm, reflective cat that loves to observe. It is not intrusive, but creates a deep bond with its adoptive family—so much so that when it feels lonely, it reacts by meowing noisily.

Magical Bond: Attributed Spiritual Qualities and Powers

The Scottish Fold is able to energetically rebalance shared environments. It brings calm, stability, and cohesion, in particular in family or community relations. It is the perfect cat for harmonizing homes in which tension is being breathed or where it is necessary to once again find an element of warmth and mutual understanding. Its energy wraps and "softens" the sharpest emotional angles, especially if next to amber, a stone that strengthens family bonds.

Relation with the Owner

For a witch, the Scottish Fold is a discreet and intuitive ally. It supports rituals of protection of the house. It is perfect for magic connected to the family nest, daily care, creation of shared sacred spaces. Its sensitivity makes it also a precious companion for working on family dynamics or to safeguard the magical energy of a personal space.

FOCUS

Scottish Fold: The Legend of Susie

IN 1961, IN A PEACEFUL SCOTTISH FARM CLOSE TO COUPAR ANGUS, A WHITE CAT WAS BORN THAT WOULD CHANGE THE FELINE STORY FOREVER: SUSIE. ITS DISTINCTIVE TRAIT WERE THE EARS FOLDED FORWARD, THE RESULT OF A SPONTANEOUS MUTATION OF THE CARTILAGE. WILLIAM ROSS, A LOCAL SHEPHERD, NOTED HER AND WAS STRUCK BY HER SWEET AND FUNNY APPEARANCE. HE OBTAINED ONE OF HER KITTENS, NAMED IT "SNOOKS," AND LAUNCHED A BREEDING PROGRAM WITH HIS WIFE MARY.

ALL THE EXISTING SCOTTISH FOLDS DESCEND FROM SUSIE. THEIR STORY IS NOT ONLY A GENETIC ANOMALY THAT TURNED INTO BEAUTY, BUT ALSO A TALE OF ATTENTION AND CARE TOWARD SOMETHING THAT IS UNIQUE.

TODAY, THIS BREED AROUSES IMMEDIATE TENDERNESS AND HAS A MAGICAL AURA: AS IF EVERY SCOTTISH FOLD WERE A CREATURE THAT HAD JUST COME OUT OF AN ILLUSTRATED BOOK FOR CHILDREN.

SELKIRK REX

ORIGIN: United States

DISTINCTIVE CHARACTERISTICS: Curly fur (longhair or shorthair); sturdy body; round head

PERSONALITY: Calm, patient, reassuring

MAGICAL POWERS: Spreads emotional stability, protects from destabilizing influences

ROLE IN MAGIC: Gentle custodian, perfect for creating protected energy spaces

Origin and History

The Selkirk Rex is a young breed, born in 1987 in Montana from a spontaneous mutation in a litter of street cats. Easily recognizable by its curly fur, it was welcomed right from the start as a symbol of sweetness and comfort, and today it is associated with a warm and reassuring energy, perfect for protecting the emotional core of the house.

Physical and Behavioral Characteristics

The Selkirk Rex has a solid and well-structured body, with a round head, sweet eyes, and soft, curly fur. It loves being around humans and other cats, but needs a space in which to withdraw in search of tranquility.

Magical Bond: Attributed Spiritual Qualities and Powers

The Selkirk Rex naturally spreads stability and affection. Its energy is enveloping, like a hug that protects and reassures. Working together with the green aventurine, a stone that protects the heart, it attracts positivity and has a calming effect on the nervous system.
It is ideal for practices of self-consolation and family harmony.

Relation with the Owner

The Selkirk Rex is a companion that offers silent and constant support. It contributes to creating a sweet, welcoming, protected magical space. It is perfect for rituals connected to the family core, self-care, and emotional protection. Its soft energy helps its human companion not become stiff, let themselves go, and feel protected when everything around is moving.

PERSIAN CAT

ORIGIN: Asia Minor

DISTINCTIVE CHARACTERISTICS: Long, thick fur; flat face; large, deep eyes

PERSONALITY: Calm, reserved, gentle

MAGICAL POWERS: Stabilizes and protects domestic energy, absorbs environmental tensions

ROLE IN MAGIC: Silent custodian, perfect for rituals of protection and centering

Origin and History

The Persian is one of the oldest and most recognizable breeds, with Turkish origins despite the fact that the name refers to Ancient Persia (current Iran). The first specimens were brought to Europe in the 17th century by Pietro della Valle, an orientalist. The Persian's regal bearing has made it, over the centuries, a preferred companion of sovereigns like Queen Victoria of the United Kingdom and Emperor Napoleon III of France.

Physical and Behavioral Characteristics

The Persian has a compact and solid body, covered by long, thick, and silky fur. Its flattened face and large eyes give it a placid and dreamy expression. It is a cat that tends to be calm, loves routine and safe places. Although it is affectionate, it is not intrusive—it offers its presence with discretion and does not like big changes within the family environment. It is perfect for those who want a sweet and silent companion.

Magical Bond: Attributed Spiritual Qualities and Powers

The Persian is considered capable of channeling the energies of calm and protection. Its magic has the purpose of improving the energy of the environment by absorbing tensions and creating a serene space. It is connected to the protection of the house, the body, and the spirit. It does not step with force, but operates in depth, offering a stable energy field.

Relation with the Owner

The Persian is a silent but present companion, which favors slow, deep, and receptive practices. Working in conjunction with smoky quartz, a stone that calms the heart and harmonizes the space, it is perfect for rituals of centering and rooting, and to strengthen the sense of security. Its presence relaxes, supports, envelops. This very cat protects without fuss, maintains its own magical space intact, and firmly safeguards what is fragile.

FOCUS

The Cat of the Courts and Chronicles

IN 1620, THE TRAVELER AND ORIENTALIST PIETRO DELLA VALLE LEFT ROME FOR THE MIDDLE EAST. AMONG MANY OTHER WONDERS, HE BROUGHT TO EUROPE LONGHAIR CATS FROM ANCIENT PERSIA. THOSE EXOTIC FELINES, ELEGANT AND REGAL IN BEARING, WERE THE ANCESTORS OF TODAY'S PERSIAN. IN THE 19TH CENTURY, THIS BREED SPREAD TO THE EUROPEAN COURTS AND BECAME SYMBOLS OF THE ARISTOCRACY. QUEEN VICTORIA OWNED SEVERAL, AND HER FAVORITE WAS NAMED WHITE HEATHER.

THE PERSIAN PARTICIPATED IN THE FIRST FELINE EXHIBIT AT THE CRYSTAL PALACE IN 1871, ESTABLISHING ITS POSITION AMONG THE "SALON CATS." APPRECIATED FOR ITS CALM TEMPERAMENT AND REFINED APPEARANCE, THE PERSIAN ALSO BECAME THE STAR OF PAINTINGS, PHOTOGRAPHS, AND STORIES. ITS STORY CROSSES ERAS AND SALONS, ALWAYS TIED TO THE IDEA OF BEAUTY TO BE CONTEMPLATED AND CUDDLED.

BOMBAY

ORIGIN: United States

DISTINCTIVE CHARACTERISTICS: Short, shiny black coat; copper or gold-colored eyes; "panther-like" appearance

PERSONALITY: Confident, vigilant, affectionate

MAGICAL POWERS: Absorbs negative energies; creates a protective shield

ROLE IN MAGIC: Silent defender, ideal for rituals of personal and environmental protection

Origin and History

The origins of the Bombay go back to the 1950s, when in the United States a black American Shorthair was bred with a Burmese to obtain a domestic cat that resembled a miniature black panther. Elegant but powerful, it is often associated with protection.
In the realm of magic, its dark coat is a symbol of energy absorption and spiritual reflection.

Physical and Behavioral Characteristics

The Bombay has a compact and muscular body, very short and shiny fur, and intense copper or gold-colored eyes. It is an affectionate cat, curious, and very aware of what is happening around it.

Magical Bond: Attributed Spiritual Qualities and Powers

The Bombay acts as a natural energy shield. It has the capacity to absorb and neutralize tensions and intrusive thoughts.
Working together with black tourmaline, a powerful psychic stone that rejects negativity, it is perfect for rituals of protections, for detachment from toxic energies, or for those who need a safe inner space to explore intense emotions.

Relation with the Owner

The Bombay is a very powerful ally in rituals of psychic defense and solitary practices. It helps its human companion maintain their center and recognize what is damaging before it takes root.
Its presence is discreet but powerful: a small domestic panther that protects and guides in silence.

BRITISH SHORTHAIR

ORIGIN: Great Britain

DISTINCTIVE CHARACTERISTICS: Stout body with short, thick fur; large, round eyes

PERSONALITY: Reserved, balanced, reliable

MAGICAL POWERS: Stabilizes the energy field, strengthens personal protection

ROLE IN MAGIC: Solid guardian, ideal for rituals of grounding and energy consolidation

Origin and History

The British Shorthair is one of the oldest breeds in Europe, a descendant of the cats brought by the Romans to Great Britain. Known for centuries as the English cat par excellence, it was appreciated for the particular color of its fur and its resemblance to the Cheshire cat of *Alice in Wonderland*. It is often associated with stability, to the sense of protection and the ability to stay calm, even at the most turbulent times.

Physical and Behavioral Characteristics

It has a robust and well-proportioned body, strong legs, full face, and velvety fur. Its round eyes (often copper or gold-colored) express a tranquil sweetness. It is not an intrusive cat, very independent but extremely loyal. It does not like unexpected changes, but is a faithful and serene companion, ideal for anyone desiring a constant feline presence.

Magical Bond: Attributed Spiritual Qualities and Powers

The British Shorthair helps its human companion stay centered at moments when they feel scattered, overloaded, or vulnerable. It does not work on intuition or emotion, but at the material level—it consolidates, reinforces, and protects. Its powers intensify when paired with hematite, the stone of energetic stability.

Relation with the Owner

For a witch, the British Shorthair is the perfect companion during rituals of grounding, financial stability, and creation of lasting intentions. Its energy is ideal for those who need reliability. It does not ask for anything, but is always there—like every true guardian.

FOCUS

British Shorthair—Between Rome and Wonderland

BROUGHT TO BRITANNIA BY THE ROMANS IN THE 1ST CENTURY AD, THE BRITISH SHORTHAIR DESCENDS FROM THE CATS THAT PROTECTED THE BARNS OF THE ENCAMPMENTS OF THE LEGIONNAIRES.
OVER TIME, THIS CAT INTERBRED WITH THE LOCAL CAT POPULATION, DEVELOPING INTO A ROBUST, COMPACT, AND RESILIENT BREED. IT HAD ALREADY BEEN RECOGNIZED AS A "BRITISH CAT" IN THE 19TH CENTURY, WHEN IT PARTICIPATED IN THE FIRST FELINE EXPOSITION OF LONDON. BUT ITS FAME GREW EVEN MORE, THANKS TO LITERATURE: THE AUTHOR LEWIS CARROLL WAS INSPIRED BY THE BRITISH SHORTHAIR TO CREATE THE CHESHIRE CAT OF "ALICE IN WONDERLAND".
THAT WIDE, MYSTERIOUS, AND PHILOSOPHICAL SMILE, CAPABLE OF DISAPPEARING, LEAVING ONLY THE MOUTH SUSPENDED IN AIR, IS THE FANTASTIC REFLECTION OF ITS CHARACTER—PRESENT BUT NEVER INTRUSIVE: AN ENIGMATIC FIGURE THAT EMBODIES THE FELINE PARADOX—TO BE AND NOT TO BE, TO APPEAR AND TO DISAPPEAR.

HIMALAYAN CAT

ORIGIN: United States

DISTINCTIVE CHARACTERISTICS: Long colorpoint fur; blue eyes; sturdy build

PERSONALITY: Affectionate, quiet, contemplative

MAGICAL POWERS: Calms mental tension, harmonizes the energies in sacred places

ROLE IN MAGIC: Ritual cat, perfect for work of meditation, beauty, and sacredness

Origin and History

The Himalayan was born from crossbreeding between a Persian and a Siamese, with the intention of combining the colorpoint elegance of the Siamese with the majesty and sweetness of the Persian. Selected at the beginning of the 20th century, today it is considered one of the most refined and esthetically harmonious breeds. Due to its combination of Eastern and Western traits, it is often associated with equilibrium between the beautiful and the sacred, and the ability to bring peace to ritual places.

Physical and Behavioral Characteristics

The body of the Himalayan is stout, with short legs, long, soft fur, and a sweet flat face, with intense blue eyes. The temperament is a union between the two breeds: on the one hand the vivacity and curiosity of the Siamese, and on the other the accommodating kindness of the Persian.

Magical Bond: Attributed Spiritual Qualities and Powers

The Himalayan transmits a contemplative energy ideal for refocusing on the heart and beauty. It is seen as a spiritual channeler, whose powers are amplified by labradorite—the magic stone that protects during inner work. Perfect for studios and meditation spaces, it is a silent companion during inner journeys.

Relation with the Owner

The Himalayan is the ideal companion during rituals of harmony and meditation practices. It brings depth without weight, stability without rigidity. It is a cat that accompanies without asking, that strengthens the connection with the calm and the sacred. During moments of meditation, it is the presence that protects the inner space.

CATS *of* TRANSFORMATION

Some cats seem to cross boundaries, moving between who we used to be and who we are becoming.

The Cats of Transformation accompany us at times of passage, when changing is not a choice but a necessity. They bring with them the energy of the renewal, the risk, the metamorphosis. We have associated two signs of the zodiac with them, which reflect the type of spiritual support given by each breed in its most diverse facets. They are spirit guides for those going through a change, for those who have chosen to go beyond their own limits, or simply for those ready to become something new.

SAVANNAH CAT

ORIGIN: United States

DISTINCTIVE CHARACTERISTICS: Wild appearance; large ears; long legs

PERSONALITY: Independent, intelligent, energetic

MAGICAL POWERS: Amplifies the sense of freedom, accelerates the evolutionary change

ROLE IN MAGIC: Guide for transformations and spiritual journeys

Origin and History

The Savannah was born from the crossbreeding of a Siamese and an African Serval. The first selective breeding dates back to the 1980s. The wild appearance and the proud disposition make it a symbol of connection with primordial instincts, as well as with the desire to explore and get beyond the limits. This cat represents the courage to expand and transform.

Physical and Behavioral Characteristics

Athletic body, sturdy framework, spotted fur, high ears: the Savannah is a concentration of wild elegance. It likes to jump, play, discover. It is very intelligent and often learns to fetch small objects or to open doors. It wants freedom but offers deep and intense affection to those who know how to respect its rhythms.

Magical Bond: Attributed Spiritual Qualities and Powers

The Savannah embodies the energy of Sagittarius—adventurous, visionary, always on a path toward new inner discoveries. It is ideal for those facing transformations that call for openness and a renewed willingness to journey—both inward and outward. It stimulates reconnection with the power to explore.

Relation with the Owner

For a witch, the Savannah is a powerful guide. It asks you to get out of your comfort zone and to reclaim your magical independence. Like the Leo, it spurs you on to recognize your personal authority and to act with pride. It is a companion that can help you during rituals to shape reality and realize your dreams.

BENGAL CAT

ORIGIN: United States

DISTINCTIVE CHARACTERISTICS: Leopard-like coat; powerful build; wild gait

PERSONALITY: Dominating, courageous, active

MAGICAL POWERS: Reawakens inner strength, stimulates courage

ROLE IN MAGIC: Perfect for rituals of liberation, renewal, and rebirth

Origin and History

The Bengal came from a crossbreeding between a domestic cat and an Asian leopard cat, with the objective of creating a breed that would unite a wild appearance with an affectionate temperament. The selective breeding began in the 1960s, but it was only in the 1980s that the breed was stabilized. Its exotic beauty and proud personality have made it a symbol of strength, audacity, and independence.

Physical and Behavioral Characteristics

Muscular, agile, with a spotted coat that resembles the jungle, the Bengal is an energetic and lively cat. It loves to explore, jump, climb. It is curious, playful, and incredibly intelligent. It needs stimulation and constant interaction, but it can also be affectionate and loyal. It is the perfect companion for those who love challenges and live change as an adventure.

Magical Bond: Attributed Spiritual Qualities and Powers

The Bengal is an activator of the inner fire. It is connected to the signs of Aries and Scorpio, two powerful and transformative archetypes of the Zodiac: the first because of its explosive energy, the second for its capacity to recover from difficult situations. The Bengal helps its human companion overcome fear, break old patterns, and forcefully launch themselves into their own evolution. It is perfect for rituals of renewal and invocations of courage.

Relation with the Owner

For a witch, the Bengal is an ally that pushes for action.
It is ideal for those who need to recover their vital energy, break toxic habits, or face radical renewal. Like Scorpio, it guides you into the depths of your shadow to make you reemerge stronger.
Like Aries, it reminds you that you have the courage to choose, act, create. It is the cat that looks you in the eye and challenges you to be authentic.

FOCUS

The Rivalry Between Cat and Mouse: A Legend as Old as the Chinese Horoscope

VARIOUS STORIES ARE ASSOCIATED WITH THE SELECTION OF THE ANIMALS THAT MAKE UP THE CHINESE HOROSCOPE. ACCORDING TO A LEGEND, BUDDHA, AWARE THAT DEATH WAS CLOSE, CALLED ALL THE ANIMALS TO HIS SIDE FOR A GREETING BEFORE CLOSING HIS EYES FOR THE LAST TIME. THE MOUSE WAS THE FIRST TO RUSH TO HIS CALL, FOLLOWED BY THE BUFFALO, TIGER, RABBIT, DRAGON, SERPENT, HORSE, GOAT, MONKEY, ROOSTER, DOG, AND PIG. WANTING TO REWARD THEIR LOYALTY, BUDDHA ESTABLISHED THAT EACH OF THESE ANIMALS WOULD GIVE ITS NAME TO A LUNAR CYCLE.

THE CAT DID NOT COME. FOR THIS REASON, ITS NAME DOES NOT APPEAR IN THE HOROSCOPE. ACCORDING TO ANOTHER LEGEND, THE JADE EMPEROR WAS ASTONISHED BY THE VARIETY OF ANIMALS LIVING ON EARTH AND DECIDED TO TAKE SOME UP TO THE SKY.

THE MOUSE, JEALOUS OF THE CAT'S BEAUTY, DIDN'T WARN HIM. WHEN THE CAT BECAME AWARE OF IT, HE GOT VERY ANGRY WITH THE RODENT.

THIS IS WHERE THE RIVALRY BETWEEN CAT AND MOUSE STARTED, AND IT STILL CONTINUES TO THE PRESENT DAY.

OCICAT

ORIGIN: United States

DISTINCTIVE CHARACTERISTICS: Spotted fur; athletic body; penetrating gaze

PERSONALITY: Curious, sociable, dynamic

MAGICAL POWERS: Stimulates creativity, encourages transformation in relations

ROLE IN MAGIC: Perfect mediator for rituals of conscious change

Origin and History

The Ocicat was born by accident in the 1960s, from a crossbreeding between a Siamese and an Abyssinian—a domestic cat with an exotic appearance and affectionate heart.
It is the perfect symbol of personal transformation: what we seem to be is not always what we are, and every real change goes by a deep understanding of ourselves.

Physical and Behavioral Characteristics

Its body is muscular and agile; the spotted coat makes it look similar to a jungle cat. The Ocicat is an affectionate, sociable cat that adapts to various contexts with extraordinary flexibility. It likes to move lightly between the house and the world outside. It has a brilliant personality and demonstrates great interest in strangers.

Magical Bond: Attributed Spiritual Qualities and Powers

The Ocicat is tied to the energy of Gemini—curious, dynamic, connected to mental change and communication abilities. Its magic consists of facilitating the evolution of the relations: connections, communications, clarifications. It is a bridge between what we were and what we want to become.

Relation with the Owner

For a witch, the Ocicat is an ally in the exploration of inner and outer change. Like Libra, it encourages harmony, but also invites ongoing self-questioning. It accompanies in rituals of openness, dialog, reconciliation.

EGYPTIAN MAU

ORIGIN: Egypt (old), United States (modern selective breeding)

DISTINCTIVE CHARACTERISTICS: Natural spotting; amber or green eyes; elegant gait

PERSONALITY: Intuitive, reserved, sensitive

MAGICAL POWERS: Awakens ancestral memory, fosters rites of transformation

ROLE IN MAGIC: Perfect for practices of connection with ancestral roots

Origin and History

The Egyptian Mau is considered the only domestic cat with natural spots. It was already regarded as sacred in Ancient Egypt, where it was venerated in the temples and often depicted next to the deities. Even though the modern selection of the breed occurred in the United States in the 20th century, the Mau still embodies today the archetype of the spiritual custodian. It is a symbol of transformation through memory: only what we honor can be faced and overcome.

Physical and Behavioral Characteristics

Elegant and powerful, the Egyptian Mau has eyes that range from amber-colored to intense green, and well-developed muscles. It is one of the fastest domestic cats. It loves to observe and explore, and it has a highly accentuated emotional sensitivity. It is selective regarding the humans which it decides to trust; but when it comes to love them it becomes a silent and profound presence, a discreet and reassuring guide.

Magical Bond: Attributed Spiritual Qualities and Powers

The Mau resounds with the energy of the Virgo, connected to purification, ritual precision, and connection with the sacredness of the Earth. It is custodian of ritual gestures. It is perfect for practices that require order, connection with the ancestors, or symbolic passages through personal limits.

Relation with the Owner

For a witch, the Mau is a sensitive and discreet companion that provides company during rites of deep transformation, in particular those connected to memory, the past, the grounding in the personal and family history. Like Cancer, it works with intimacy, emotional memory, the inner house. It is ideal for those who want to transform nostalgia in awareness, the wounds in wisdom.

FOCUS

A "Divine" Cat

THE EGYPTIAN MAU AND THE ABYSSINIAN ARE THE OLDEST DOMESTIC CATS: SOME DEPICTIONS OF THESE CATS HAVE BEEN FOUND ON EGYPTIAN TOMBS DATING BACK TO THE 16TH CENTURY B.C. GRAIN WAS ONE OF THE PRINCIPAL SOURCES OF SUSTENANCE IN ANCIENT EGYPT; FOR THIS REASON, THE PRESENCE OF FELINES TO AVOID VISITS BY UNDESIRABLE RATS IN THE BARNS WAS INDISPENSABLE. ITS ROLE WAS SO IMPORTANT THAT THERE WAS A SERIES OF LAWS DRAFTED TO PROTECT IT.

ANY ACT OF VIOLENCE AGAINST CATS WAS PROHIBITED, AND EVEN MORE PROHIBITED WAS TAKING THEM OUTSIDE THE BORDERS OF THE KINGDOM. TRANSGRESSORS WOULD FACE VERY SEVERE PENALTIES. IN ADDITION, THERE WAS THE BELIEF THAT THE EGYPTIAN MAU WAS ENDOWED WITH MAGICAL POWERS: ON ITS FOREHEAD THERE IS A PATTERN THAT RECALLS FROM AFAR THE SACRED SCARAB. THIS SAME SCARAB APPEARS ON THE FOREHEADS OF THE FELINES DEPICTED IN THE TEMPLES, AND THEREFORE INDICATES A CONNECTION WITH THE DIVINE.

PETERBALD

ORIGIN: Russia

DISTINCTIVE CHARACTERISTICS: Hairless or with very short fur; elongated profile; elegant appearance

PERSONALITY: Lively, brilliant, affectionate

MAGICAL POWERS: Stimulates intuitive creativity, leads to inner rebirth

ROLE IN MAGIC: Subtle innovator, perfect for rituals of breaking and transformation

Origin and History

The Peterbald is a recent breed, developed in the 1990s in Saint Petersburg. It comes from crossbreeding the Donskoy and the Oriental Shorthair. Its futuristic appearance, its intelligence, and its sensitivity make it a cat with an almost alien aura: not only outside the box, but bearer of new visions. It is the symbol of change that is not afraid to step outside the reassuringly familiar space.

Physical and Behavioral Characteristics

Elegant, slender, and muscular, the Peterbald can be hairless or have a light veil of fur. It has magnetic eyes, large ears, a harmonious gait. It is very affectionate and needs human contact, but retains a curious and lively mind. It loves communication and does not hesitate to "chat" with its human companion.

Magical Bond: Attributed Spiritual Qualities and Powers

The Peterbald embodies the energies of Aquarius—anti-conformist and innovative. It is perfect for those who are changing their way of living, thinking, being. It fosters rituals of liberation from obsolete mental boxes and reconnection with the authentic being.

Relation with the Owner

For a witch, the Peterbald is a support in the transition.
It accompanies you at times of crisis that anticipate a rebirth. Like Pisces, it has a thin sensitivity, almost psychic—it captures emotions and the soul, stimulates dreams and visions. It is ideal for practices connected to intuitive creativity.

JAPANESE BOBTAIL (SHORTHAIR)

ORIGIN: Japan

DISTINCTIVE CHARACTERISTICS: Short and curly tail; slender body; agile and harmonious movements

PERSONALITY: Balanced, curious, joyful

MAGICAL POWERS: Brings fortune and continuity, facilitates the slow steps of change

ROLE IN MAGIC: Spiritual guide, ideal for rituals of consolidation and deep and challenging transformations

Origin and History

The Japanese Bobtail is an ancient Asian breed, very present in Japanese culture, where it is a symbol of good luck.
It appears in numerous prints and sculptures, and is depicted in the *maneki neko*, the cats with the raised paw that bring prosperity.
Its naturally short tail makes it unique. This cat is a symbol of serene transformation. It encourages changes that come with grace and respect for values.

Physical and Behavioral Characteristics

It is characterized by an agile and muscular body, and a silky coat. Its tail, similar to a small pom-pom, is unmistakable. The Japanese Bobtail is a curious, playful, and very intelligent cat, so much so that it learns its name and answers when called. It loves routine as much as discovery, maintains a perfect balance between dynamism and stability. It brings joy, harmony, and lightness to life's transitions.

Magical Bond: Attributed Spiritual Qualities and Powers

This cat is in resonance with Taurus—slow but constant, it loves well-being and grounding. It is a guide for the changes that require patience, constancy, and care. It is ideal for those going through a process of evolution made of small steps, daily construction, and conscious change.

Relation with the Owner

For a witch, the Japanese Bobtail is a support that accompanies with grace and determination. Like Capricorn, it is not in a hurry but goes all the way. It supports you in long-term projects, in deep but measured transformations. It is perfect for rituals of responsible growth, construction, and protection of a magic journey.

FOCUS

Maneki Neko: A Fortunate Feline

THE JAPANESE BOBTAIL IS SEEN AS AN ACTUAL SOURCE OF GOOD FORTUNE IN THE LAND OF THE RISING SUN.
THE STORY GOES THAT IN 999 AD, THESE CATS ARRIVED IN JAPAN FROM CHINA, AND WERE FOR A LONG TIME CONSIDERED THE PERFECT ANIMAL FOR NOBLE FAMILIES.
IN PARTICULAR, THE SHORT-TAILED CATS GAINED A SPECIAL PLACE IN THE HEARTS OF THE JAPANESE PEOPLE.
AN ANCIENT LEGEND SPOKE OF THE TERRIBLE OKABE DEMON CAT, RECOGNIZABLE BY ITS FORKED TAIL.
HAVING A TAIL THAT IS NEITHER LONG NOR FORKED LIKE THE DEMON'S, AND WHICH MOREOVER LOOKED LIKE A CHRYSANTHEMUM FLOWER, SYMBOL OF THE EMPEROR AND THE IMPERIAL FAMILY, THE BOBTAIL SOON BECAME THE NATIONAL CAT OF JAPAN. SO MUCH SO THAT IT IS PORTRAYED IN THE *MANEKI NEKO*, A LUCKY CHARM WITH A SMALL BELL AROUND ITS NECK AND A RAISED PAW, AS IF IN THE ACT OF IMPARTING A BLESSING.

HAVANA BROWN

ORIGIN: United Kingdom

DISTINCTIVE CHARACTERISTICS: Shiny brown coat; elongated face; light green eyes

PERSONALITY: Energetic, thoughtful, magnetic

MAGICAL POWERS: Reawakens the desire for authenticity, transforms energy into personal power

ROLE IN MAGIC: Channeler of awareness and inner strength, ideal for rites of passage

Origin and History

The Havana Brown was born in the United Kingdom in the middle of the 20th century from a planned crossbreeding between Siamese and domestic black cats. It is a breed of unmistakable beauty. Its intense chocolate color and its sober elegance make it a magnetic cat, with an almost esoteric fascination. It is an animal that does not go unnoticed, and still today is regarded as a rarity.

Physical and Behavioral Characteristics

Its body is elegant, lean, with a shiny coat that is unique in its kind. The green eyes convey deep attention. The Havana Brown is an affectionate but selective cat, thoughtful but decisive. It does not look for attention: it attracts it naturally. It loves to play, although it cyclically needs moments of solitude and quiet.

Magical Bond: Attributed Spiritual Qualities and Powers

This cat has the same energy as Scorpio, which digs, reprocesses, and transforms. The Havana Brown is not afraid of the shadow: it inhabits it and models it as it wants. It is perfect for rituals of regeneration and renewal of personal power.

Relation with the Owner

For a witch, the Havana Brown is a guide in the journey for the quest of the true essence. Like Leo, it helps its human companion shine without appeasing, to establish themselves with authenticity. It is ideal for those emerging from a period of uncertainty or subordination, and wants to affirm its presence with force and awareness. It is a companion in the rites of personal identity and centering.

CATS *of* FORTUNE

There are cats that seem to bring with them breath of blessing, creatures capable of attracting fortunate occasions, happy relations, and small daily miracles.

The Cats of Fortune embody the energy of personal development, joy, and meaningful synchronicities. We have associated with each of them planets of astrology that amplify magical and symbolic qualities—the abundance of Jupiter, the sweetness of Venus, the transformative strength of Pluto, the emotional nature of the Moon. These felines are perfect companions for those wishing to cultivate the beauty of life, to accept the chance, and to open up to a fortune created with passion.

LYKOI

ORIGIN: United States

DISTINCTIVE CHARACTERISTICS: Thin or patchy coat; "werewolf" appearance; almond-shaped eyes

PERSONALITY: Sharp, curious, independent

MAGICAL POWERS: Encourages deep transformation, stimulates mental adaptability

ROLE IN MAGIC: Cat of rebirth, ideal for rituals of development and inner reawakening

Origin and History

The Lykoi, the "werewolf cat," is a recent breed born from a natural mutation discovered in the United States in 2010. Its distinctive feature is its irregular coat, composed of black and white fur, which gives it a wild and ancient appearance. Associated right from the start with the idea of metamorphosis, the Lykoi has become a powerful symbol of radical change, of acceptance of imperfection, and of awakening of the hidden identity.

Physical and Behavioral Characteristics

The Lykoi is a slender and surprisingly agile cat. It easily adapts to different contexts, carefully observes its surroundings, and carefully chooses whom to trust. Despite its wild appearance, it can establish a deep bond with those who respect its independence.

Magical Bond: Attributed Spiritual Qualities and Powers

The Lykoi is closely linked to Pluto, the planet of transformation and hidden power. It is a catalyst of deep changes, supporting the capacity to let the old go and to be reborn in a new energy form. Like Mercury, it stimulates quick reflexes and thinking.

Relation with the Owner

For a witch, the Lykoi is a guide during rites of personal development and awakening of the true nature of self. It is perfect in rituals of metamorphosis, transition, and discovery of the deepest authenticity. Its presence is also of great help in rituals to facilitate communication, trade, and study.

MANX CAT

ORIGIN: Isle of Man

DISTINCTIVE CHARACTERISTICS: No tail or a very short tail; compact body; peculiar gait

PERSONALITY: Protective, playful, strong bond with the house

MAGICAL POWERS: Brings prosperity, protects the house and its inhabitants

ROLE IN MAGIC: Good-luck guardian, ideal for rites of abundance and domestic blessing

Origin and History

The Manx is originally from the Isle of Man in the Irish Sea, where it developed naturally with the genetic characteristic of its missing tail. Fascinating legends have arisen around this particularity, connected both to Biblical events and the ancient barbarian populations that inhabited the island. Always seen as a source of good fortune, it is tied to the maritime tradition as protector of travelers and domestic spaces.

Physical and Behavioral Characteristics

The Manx is a sturdy cat, compact, with rear legs longer than the front ones, which gives it a gait and appearance almost like a rabbit. It is joyful, affectionate, loyal, and very tied to its territory. It loves the family environment, to which it adapts relatively easily, and it keeps a close watch over the house.

Magical Bond: Attributed Spiritual Qualities and Powers

The Manx is deeply connected to the Moon, the star of intuition, the house, and the cyclical way of life. It is the cat that protects the domestic fortune, protects the family bonds, and strengthens them. Like Jupiter, the planet of expansion and growth, it amplifies whatever good is cultivated, protects from what is unnecessary, and encourages abundance in the small things of everyday life.

Relation with the Owner

For a witch, the Manx is a productive and discreet guardian. It acts as support during the rituals of wealth, emotional protection, internal stability, and gratitude. Its presence attracts good fortune, emotional security, and abundance like the phase of the crescent moon.

FOCUS

An Unfortunate Incident on Noah's Ark

THE SEVERED OR TOTALLY MISSING TAIL OF THE MANX HAS ALWAYS STOKED LEGENDS REGARDING ITS ORIGINS. IT IS SAID THAT THIS CAT WAS THE LAST TO REACH NOAH'S ARK TO SAVE ITSELF FROM THE FLOOD, ENDING UP WITH ITS TAIL TRAPPED IN THE DOOR, WHICH CUT IT OFF COMPLETELY. BUT THERE ARE EVEN BLOODIER STORIES REGARDING THE MISSING APPENDIX OF THE POOR FELINE: ANOTHER LEGEND SAYS THAT THE BARBARIANS WHO INHABITED THE ISLE OF MAN LIKED TO CUT OFF THE TAILS OF THE CATS AND DECORATE THEIR HELMETS WITH THEM AS A SIGN OF VICTORY. CONSEQUENTLY, THE MOTHER CATS STARTED TO DOCK THE TAIL OF THEIR OWN LITTLE ONES TO AVOID THEIR BEING CAPTURED AND MISTREATED BY THE BARBARIANS.

SNOWSHOE CAT

ORIGIN: United States

DISTINCTIVE CHARACTERISTICS: White paws; blue eyes; elegant and compact body

PERSONALITY: Gentle, sensitive, well balanced

MAGICAL POWERS: Reinforces emotional resilience, encourages harmony and relational fortune

ROLE IN MAGIC: Builder of bridges, ideal for rituals of stability and emotional prosperity

Origin and History

The Showshoe was born in the 1960s in the United States from a crossbreeding between a Siamese and an American Shorthair. Its distinctive characteristic are its white paws, which look like snowshoes. This breed is linked to symbolisms of protection, aimed at facilitating a personal journey—every step is light but leaves a significant mark. It is seen as a bearer of balance between strength and sweetness.

Physical and Behavioral Characteristics

The Snowshoe combines the slender elegance of the Siamese with the softer sweetness typical of the American Shorthair. Generally, it loves the company of humans that share its love for tranquility. Also for this reason, we do not recommend the Snowshoe as a companion for very small children, since this breed does not like noise and confusion very much.

Magical Bond: Attributed Spiritual Qualities and Powers

The Snowshoe is associated with Saturn, the planet of solidity and wisdom created over time. Like Venus, it protects emotional bonds and fosters balance in everyday relations.

Relation with the Owner

For a witch, the Snowshoe is a companion that brings beauty and harmony. It is ideal for rituals dedicated to sensuality, lasting love, and the construction of tangible happiness. Its energy teaches to cultivate joy in everyday actions, and to build fortune on solid foundations, without rushing but with determination.

MUNCHKIN CAT

ORIGIN: United States

DISTINCTIVE CHARACTERISTICS: Short legs; elongated body; playful gait

PERSONALITY: Cheerful, curious, energetic

MAGICAL POWERS: Brings lightness and open-mindedness, favors unexpected fortune

ROLE IN MAGIC: Messenger of opportunity, ideal for rituals of positive change

Origin and History

The Munchkin is a recent breed that appeared in the United States in the 1980s, after a natural mutation which gives these cats their characteristic short legs. The name is inspired by the little Munchkins of "The Wonderful Wizard of Oz." Their peculiarity does not slow them down: on the contrary, they express energy, adaptability, and an extraordinary capacity to transform every limit into a strength.

Physical and Behavioral Characteristics

Despite its short legs, the Munchkin is agile, quick, and very curious. It has an elongated body, a toned musculature, and an extroverted nature. It loves to explore, play, interact.

It is friendly, intelligent, and able to adapt quickly to changes, instilling a sense of dynamism and lightness into domestic life.

Magical Bond: Attributed Spiritual Qualities and Powers

The Munchkin is associated with Mercury, the planet of communication and mental agility. Like Jupiter, the planet of expansion and growth, it opens us up to unexpected possibilities and favors the manifestation of fortunate opportunities.

Relation with the Owner

For a witch, the Munchkin is an ally of growth and joy.

It is perfect in rituals of success, transcendence, and attracting good fortune. It carries the magic of dynamism and creativity, inspires positive transformation, and sharpens the ability to seize opportunities as they arise—even the most unexpected.

FOCUS

A Marvelous (Feline) World of Oz

THE MUNCHKIN CAT GETS ITS NAME FROM THE CHARACTERS WITH THE SAME NAME THAT POPULATE THE MUNCHKINLAND, IN THE CHILDREN'S BOOK "THE WONDERFUL WIZARD OF OZ" BY L. FRANK BAUM, AN AMERICAN WRITER AND FILM PRODUCER WHO LIVED FROM THE SECOND HALF OF THE 19TH CENTURY THROUGH THE FIRST QUARTER OF THE 20TH CENTURY.
THE INHABITANTS OF THE WORLD OF OZ, WHO LITTLE DOROTHY MEETS AT THE START OF HER VOYAGE LOOKING FOR THE WIZARD, HAVE A LOT IN COMMON WITH THE CAT WITH THE SAME NAME. LIKE IT, THEY ARE FRIENDLY AND AFFECTIONATE, AND THEY NATURALLY SHARE A SMALL SIZE. ANOTHER PECULIARITY OF THIS CAT IS ITS ABILITY TO SIT ON ITS BACK PAWS, SUPPORTING ITSELF WITH ITS TAIL, AND MOVING ITS FRONT PAWS LIKE A KANGAROO.